LAUGH
-OUT-
LOUD

THE
1,001 FUNNIEST
LOL JOKES
OF ALL TIME

LAUGH
-OUT-
LOUD

THE
1,001 FUNNIEST
LOL JOKES
OF ALL TIME

ROB ELLIOTT

HARPER

An Imprint of HarperCollinsPublishers

Library of Congress Control Number: 2021935319
ISBN 978-0-06-308062-1

21 22 23 24 25 PC/LSCH 10 9 8 7 6 5 4 3 2 1

First Edition

Q: What did one marshmallow say to the other?

A: "I want s'more time with you!"

Q: How did the zookeeper calm down the wild elephant?

A: With a trunk-quilizer.

Q: Why were there lizards all over the bathroom wall?

A: Because it had been rep-tiled.

Q: Why did the man cry when he ran out of cola?

A: Because it was soda-pressing.

Q: How are bus drivers like trees?

A: They both have routes.

Q: Why did the clock go on vacation?

A: It needed to unwind.

Q: What does a duck wear to its wedding?

A: A ducks-edo!

Q: What does a Tyrannosaurus rex eat while it's camping?

A: Dino-s'mores!

Q: Why did the bee marry the rabbit?

A: She was his honey bunny.

Q: What do sheep always take on camping trips?

A: Their baa-ckpacks.

Q: What do you call a squid with only six arms?

A: A hexa-pus.

Q: **Why can't you take a skunk on vacation?**

A: Your trip will stink!

Q: **What do you call the worm that ate Beethoven?**

A: A de-composer.

Q: **Why should you always listen to porcupines?**

A: They have a lot of good points.

Q: **What do you get when you cross a carrot and a pair of scissors?**

A: Par-snips.

Q: Why don't sand dollars take baths?

A: Because they wash up on the shore.

Q: Why did the boy and girl play tennis on their date?

A: It was a court-ship.

Andy: Did you hear about the panther that told the boy he wouldn't eat him?

Daniel: No, what happened?

Andy: He was lion.

Q: Why did the butcher work so hard?

A: He had to bring home the bacon.

Q: What goes up and down but never moves?

A: A flight of stairs.

Q: How much does it cost to become an electrician?

A: There's no charge.

Q: How do crabs buy their toys?

A: With sand dollars.

Q: What kind of pole can't you climb?

A: A tadpole.

Q: Why wouldn't the jellyfish go down the water slide?

A: Because he was spineless.

Q: How did the farmer show his wife he loved her?

A: He brought home the bacon.

Q: What does a trash collector eat for lunch?

A: Junk food.

- -

Q: What did the man do when he was standing out in a thunderstorm?

A: He hailed a cab.

Q: Why did the mummy keep hugging her kids goodbye?

A: She thought they were eerie-sistible.

Q: Do turkeys like to eat hot lunch?

A: Yes, they gobble it right up.

Q: What do spiders eat at a picnic?

A: Corn on the cobweb.

Q: Why was the butterfly embarrassed when it came to the dance?

A: Because it was a moth ball.

Q: What happened when the beagle played in the snow?

A: It turned into a chili dog!

Q: How do gardeners kiss?

A: With their tulips.

Q: Why wouldn't the cow get a job?

A: Because he was a meat loafer.

Q: What do you get if you put a pig on a racetrack?

A: A road hog!

Q: What do you call a crocodile that's always picking fights?

A: An insti-gator.

Q: What do whales eat for a snack?

A: Ships and salsa.

Q: Where does a sailor go when he's sick?

A: To the dock.

Q: Why did the robin get a library card?

A: It was hoping to find some bookworms.

Q: Why did the pilot paint his jet?

A: He thought it was too plane.

Q: What did the girl snake say to the boy snake?

A: "Will you be my boa-friend?"

Q: How do artists get to work?

A: They go over the drawbridge.

Q: Where do tarantulas get their

information?

A: From the World Wide Web.

Q: Why do cows believe everything

you say?

A: Because they're so gulli-bull.

Q: What's a pirate's favorite subject?

A: Arrr-ithmetic.

Q: Why did the whale buy a violin?

A: So it could join the orca-stra.

Q: What kind of bugs weigh less every day?

A: Lightening bugs.

Q: Why did the meteorite go to Hollywood?

A: It wanted to be a star.

Q: Why don't polar bears and penguins fall in love?

A: Because they're polar opposites.

Q: What do you call a hamburger in space?

A: A meat-eor!

Luke: I'm so tired of climbing this big hill!

Zack: Oh, get over it!

Q: Why don't turtles use the drive-through?

A: They don't like fast food.

Q: How do the basketball players stay cool during games?

A: They sit by their fans.

Q: Where do elephants keep their spare tires?

A: In their trunks.

Q: What falls down but never gets hurt?

A: Raindrops!

Q: How did the lettuce win the race?

A: It got a head start!

Q: What happened when the vampire met his blind date?

A: It was love at first bite.

Q: Why didn't the melons get married?

A: Because they cantaloupe.

Q: What kind of shoes do ninjas wear?

A: Sneakers.

Q: How does Saturn clean its rings?

A: With a meteor shower!

Q: What is the best way to get straight A's in school?

A: Use a ruler.

Q: When do scuba divers sleep underwater?

A: When they're snore-kling.

Q: Why wouldn't the earthworm play outside?

A: It was grounded.

Q: Why did the mechanic stop pumping gas?

A: It was a tank-less job.

Q: Why shouldn't you date a sausage?

A: Because they're the wurst!

Q: What's a tornado's favorite game?

A: Twister!

Q: How did the monkey escape from the zoo?

A: In a hot-air baboon.

Q: What is something you always leave behind at the beach?

A: Your footprints.

Q: Why did the textbook go to the hospital?

A: It needed its appendix taken out.

Q: How are flowers like the letter *A*?

A: Bees come after them.

Q: What does a wasp wear when it's raining?

A: A yellow jacket.

Q: Why do dogs have a great attitude?

A: They like to stay paws-itive.

Q: Why did the turtle have a bad time with her date?

A: He wouldn't come out of his shell.

Q: What kind of bugs like sushi?

A: Wasa-bees.

- -

Q: Why did the pelican run out of money?

A: It had a big bill.

Q: What did the ocean do when the kids left the beach?

A: It waved goodbye.

Q: Why did the library book go to the chiropractor?

A: It needed its spine adjusted.

Q: Why do sharks swim in salt water?

A: Pepper water makes them sneeze!

Q: Why do potatoes make good detectives?

A: They keep their eyes peeled.

Q: What do they eat in the Navy?

A: Submarine sandwiches.

Q: What did the snakes do after their fight?

A: They hissed and made up.

Q: Why do wasps need to go on vacation?

A: Because they're always busy bees.

Q: **How do you make a strawberry shake?**

A: Tell it a scary story.

Q: **Why did the surfer go to the hair salon?**

A: She wanted a permanent wave.

Q: **Why are clarinet players so smart?**

A: Because they reed a lot!

Q: **What's a frog's favorite kind of music?**

A: Hip-hop!

Q: How does a bison pay for dinner and a movie?

A: It uses buffalo bills.

Q: What do you get when you cross a strawberry with a propeller?

A: A jelly-copter!

Q: What do you get when a butcher and a baker get married?

A: Meat loaf.

Q: What do you get when you cross a king with a boat?

A: Leadership!

Q: Why did the berry go out with the fig?

A: Because it couldn't get a date.

Tom: Hey, want to hear another insect joke?

Jim: No, stop bugging me!

Rita: Do you know where they cooked the first French fries?

Stephanie: France?

Rita: No, in Greece!

Sam: Why did the alien grow a garden in space?

Marcus: It had a green thumb!

Q: What do you call it when two boats fall in love?

A: A relation-ship.

Q: Why is it hard to be a firefighter?

A: You get fired every day!

Q: How do mountains stay warm in the winter?

A: With their snowcaps.

Q: How do you send a knight on a mission?

A: You give him a re-quest.

Q: Why wouldn't the acrobat perform in winter?

A: He only knew how to do summer-saults.

Q: How do bees fix their hair?

A: With a honey-comb.

Q: What do you get when you cross a crocodile and a GPS?

A: A navi-gator.

Q: Why were the goats sent to the principal's office?

A: They kept butting heads.

Q: What is a beluga's favorite drink?

A: Mana-tea.

Q: Where do tarantulas look for love?

A: On dating web-sites.

Q: Where do pirates go to the bathroom?

A: On the poop deck.

Q: How did the polar bear get to work?

A: On a motor-icicle.

Q: Why did the beaver cross the road?

A: To get to the otter side.

Q: What goes up when the rain comes down?

A: An umbrella.

Q: What happens when a toad is nervous?

A: It gets worry warts!

Q: Why did the chicken run onto the soccer field?

A: Because the ref called fowl.

Q: How do fish get around the busy ocean?

A: They hail a crab.

Q: What did the stamp say to the envelope?

A: "I'm stuck on you."

Q: Why did the lumberjack fall asleep?

A: He was board!

Q: **What do you get when your dad rides a bike?**

A: A pop-cycle.

Q: **Why was the tightrope walker stressed out?**

A: He was having trouble balancing his schedule.

Q: **What kind of bow can't you tie?**

A: A rainbow.

Q: **What do you get when you cross a cow with a roll of tape?**

A: A beef stick.

Q: Why don't bumblebees drink coffee before they go to school?

A: They get too buzzed!

Q: How does the sun kiss the moon?

A: It puckers its ec-lipse.

Q: Why did the noses break up?

A: They kept picking on each other.

Q: What do you call tiny glasses?

A: Speck-tacles.

Q: What do you call a dancing sheep?

A: A baaa-llerina.

Q: When is a boxer a comedian?

A: When he delivers a punch line!

Q: Why did the skunk become a police officer?

A: It believed in law and odor.

Q: Why do skunks always show off?

A: They want to be the scent-er of attention.

Q: What do groundhogs like to read?

A: Pop-up books.

Q: What kind of bird do you send on a quest?

A: A knight owl.

Q: Why did the meteorologist cancel her date?

A: She was feeling under the weather.

Q: What do you get when you throw cabbage in the snow?

A: Cold slaw.

Q: Why did the cow become an acrobat?

A: It was so flexi-bull!

Q: **What do you get when a witch loses her magic?**

A: A hex-a-gone.

Q: **What do you call an angry vegetable?**

A: A grum-pea!

Q: **Why don't canaries want to pay for a vacation?**

A: Because they're cheep!

Q: **Why did the librarian wear sparkly purple glasses?**

A: She wanted to make a spectacle of herself.

Q: What kind of lion can you let in the house?

A: A dande-lion!

Q: How did the broom know it was in love?

A: It was swept off its feet.

Q: Where do you take a fish for an operation?

A: To the sturgeon.

Q: Where do tropical fish keep their work?

A: In a reef-case.

Q: What do you eat for lunch in the desert?

A: Sand-wiches.

Q: Where do trees go when they are tired?

A: For-rest.

Q: What goes tick, tick, woof, woof?

A: A watchdog.

Q: Where do they make all the books for school?

A: In a fact-ory.

Q: What do you get when you combine a snail and a porcupine?

A: A slowpoke!

Q: What happened to the atoms when they got in fight?

A: They split up!

Q: What happens if a kangaroo can't jump?

A: It feels un-hoppy.

Q: What do bananas and acrobats have in common?

A: They can both do splits.

Q: When can't you trust a painter?

A: When he's a con artist.

Q: What kinds of birds are never happy?

A: Bluebirds.

Q: Why didn't the man trust his bushes?

A: They seemed shady.

Q: Why was the nose feeling sad at school?

A: It kept getting picked on.

Q: What kind of candy do boxers eat?

A: Jawbreakers!

Q: Why did the tailor and the quilter get married?

A: Because they were sew in love!

Susie: Want to go see the llamas?

Sofia: That sounds fun!

Susie: Alpaca suitcase.

Q: Why can't you give your dog the TV remote?

A: It'll keep hitting the paws button.

Q: How does a slug cross the ocean?

A: In a snailboat!

Q: When is a snail the life of the party?

A: When it comes out of its shell.

Q: What happened when the duck went to the doctor?

A: It got a clean bill of health.

Q: What do sea turtles like to study?

A: Current events.

Q: Why is it hard to beat a barber in a race?

A: They take shortcuts!

Q: Why do baseball players always take their dates to restaurants?

A: They like to stay behind the plate.

Q: Where does a rabbit go when he needs glasses?

A: A hop-thalmologist.

Q: Why did the snail take a nap?

A: It was feeling sluggish.

Q: When do bees keep you healthy?

A: When they're vitamin B's.

Q: Where does a peach take a nap?

A: On an apri-cot.

Q: Why did the student throw the calendar out the window?

A: To make the days fly by.

Q: What do boxers eat for dinner?

A: Black-eyed peas.

Q: What do you call a sleepy woodcutter?

A: A slumber-jack.

Q: What kind of dog is always sad?

A: A melon-collie.

Q: What did the horse say when its date didn't show up for dinner?

A: "That's the last straw!"

Q: What kind of bread is the cheapest?

A: Pumper-nickel.

Q: Why do seeds make great friends?

A: They're always rooting for you!

Q: What kind of cheese stays by itself?

A: Prov-alone.

Q: What is the difference between students and fish?

A: Students love Fridays and fish hate fry-days!

Q: What do you call a cow with a telescope?

A: A star grazer.

Jim: I want to canoe down the river today.

Sue: You otter do that!

Q: What do clowns eat for lunch?

A: Peanut butter and jolly sandwiches.

Q: Why was the climbing rope anxious?

A: It was getting all strung out!

Q: What do a dog and a watch have in common?

A: They both have ticks.

Q: What kind of vegetable is hot and cold at the same time?

A: A chilly pepper.

Q: What did the hen say to its chick?

A: "You're a good egg."

Q: Why did the farmer study geometry?

A: He already had a pro-tractor!

Q: What do TVs wear to the beach?

A: Sun-screen.

Q: What do you call two birds in love?

A: Tweet-hearts.

Q: What's a bunny's favorite toy?

A: A hula hop.

Q: Why was the scuba diver embarrassed?

A: He saw the ocean's bottom.

Q: What's a farmer's favorite movie?

A: Beauty and the Beets.

Q: Why did the bee go to the allergist?

A: It had hives.

Q: What do you call songs you compose in bed?

A: Sheet music.

Q: Why did the thermometer go back to college?

A: It wanted another degree.

Q: Why did the shark cross the road?

A: To get to the other tide.

Q: What did one leaf say to the other leaf?

A: "I think I'm falling for you."

Q: Why did the butcher follow the detective?

A: He wanted to go on a steak-out.

Q: Why wouldn't the chicken grow?

A: It had smallpox.

Q: What did the dog have to do before going out to play?

A: Ask its paw first.

Q: How does a boy let you know he called?

A: He leaves a voice male.

Q: Why did the pineapple cake turn upside down?

A: It saw the cinnamon roll!

Q: **Why can't you take your hamster to school?**

A: They don't make backpacks that small.

Hannah: There's an octopus in my bathtub!

Olivia: You're just squid-ing me!

Q: **What did the baker say on her wedding day?**

A: "I loaf you with all my heart!"

Q: **What do you give a farmer who sings out of tune?**

A: A pitchfork.

Q: Why couldn't the oyster talk?

A: It clammed up!

Q: What is a penguin's favorite vegetable?

A: Snow peas.

Q: Why was the cook fired from the sandwich shop?

A: He couldn't cut the mustard!

Amy: What kind of nut do you like in your trail mix?

Susy: Cashew.

Amy: Bless you!

Laura: My pickles won a blue ribbon at the fair!

Mary: That's a very big dill!

Q: What did one magnet say to the other magnet?

A: "I'm very attracted to you!"

Q: What is a shark's favorite game show?

A: Whale of Fortune.

Q: Why did the baker become an actor?

A: He wanted to play a roll.

Q: Why did the vampire join the circus?

A: He wanted to be an acro-bat.

Q: Why can't a scarecrow be a comedian?

A: Its jokes are too corny.

Joe: Why did you put a kazoo in your lunch box?

Jim: I wanted a hum sandwich!

Q: Why didn't Jenny go to the library?

A: She was already booked!

Q: Why did the monkey need some R & R?

A: He was going bananas!

Q: How did the fisherman meet new people?

A: He net-worked.

Q: What is the richest bird?

A: An ost-rich.

Paul: Do you want to try fencing with me?

Pete: I'll take a stab at it.

Q: What is a plumber's favorite vegetable?

A: A leek!

Q: What did the alien say to the soda?

A: "Take me to your liter."

Q: Why couldn't Jake join the track team?

A: There were too many hurdles.

Q: What do you call a polar bear that makes coffee?

A: A bear-ista.

Q: **What did the cheese say to his bride?**

A: "I want to grow mold together."

Q: **How did the flea get from one dog to the other?**

A: It itch-hiked!

Q: **How does a polar bear build its house?**

A: Igloos it together.

Q: **Why can't a giraffe's tongue be twelve inches long?**

A: Because then it would be a foot!

Q: Why was the strawberry stressed out?

A: It was in a jam!

Q: What do you get if your dad gets stuck in the freezer?

A: A Pop-sicle.

Q: What do cows like to play at recess?

A: Dodge-bull.

Q: What is the noisiest animal to own?

A: A trum-pet!

Q: What did the boa constrictor say to the mouse?

A: "I think I have a crush on you!"

Q: What did the star say to the moon?

A: "I'm falling for you!"

Q: Why did the lumberjack get fired?

A: He axed too many questions.

Q: When is your mother like a window?

A: When she's being trans-parent.

Q: Why did the grape go to bed?

A: It ran out of juice!

Q: Why should you keep a whale happy?

A: If it's sad, it'll start blubbering.

Q: What do conductors and mountain climbers have in common?

A: They both like the terrain.

Q: Why did the criminal duck?

A: The judge said he was going to throw the book at him!

Q: What do rabbits play at recess?

A: Hopscotch.

Q: Why was the girl jump-roping down the hall?

A: She was skipping class.

Q: What did the apple say to the banana?

A: "I think you're ap-peeling!"

Q: When does a gorilla put on a suit?

A: When it's got monkey business!

Q: What is the most famous kind of drink?

A: A celebri-tea!

Q: What is a hippo's favorite vegetable?

A: Zoo-cchini.

Q: Why do melons stay single?

A: Because they cantaloupe.

Q: What vegetable do they serve in prison?

A: Cell-ery.

Q: What is the smartest state in America?

A: Alabama, because it has four A's and a B.

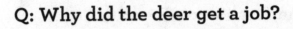

Q: Why did the deer get a job?

A: It wanted to make a quick buck.

Q: Why did the collie break up with the German shepherd?

A: It wanted to paws from dating for a while.

Q: What happened when the witch lost control of her broom?

A: She flew off the handle.

Q: How did the fisherman finish in half the time?

A: He was e-fish-ent!

Q: Why did the trombone player try to play his friend's trumpet?

A: His teacher said it's rude to toot your own horn!

Q: What don't grizzlies wear shoes?

A: They like to go bear-foot.

Q: Why did the student bring his stilts to school?

A: For show and tall.

Q: Why was the weatherman so upset?

A: Somebody stole his thunder.

- -

Q: Why did the slug break up with the snail?

A: The relationship was moving too slow.

Q: Why will a squirrel always keep a secret?

A: It's a tough nut to crack!

Q: How do snowmen stay warm at night?

A: With a blanket of snow.

James: Did you hear the joke about the hot-air balloon?

Jack: It went right over my head!

Q: Why did the cucumber call for help?

A: It was in a pickle.

Q: Why did the boy call the fire department?

A: His money was burning a hole in his pocket!

Q: Where do cows eat their lunch?

A: In the calf-eteria.

Q: Why didn't the corn take a plane?

A: Its ears would pop!

Q: Why did the candies fall in love?

A: They were mint for each other.

Q: What do you do if your walls are cold?

A: Put on another coat of paint!

Q: What do you get if you put coffee on your head?

A: A cap-puccino.

Q: What does a queen wear in a thunderstorm?

A: A reign-coat!

Tailor: Do you like your new suit?

Customer: It's sew-sew.

Q: Why did the captain quit her job?

A: Because her ship came in.

Q: Why was the clock looking forward to spring break?

A: It needed to unwind.

Q: Why don't snakes know how much they weigh?

A: They're always losing their scales.

Q: **What did the boy cat say to the girl cat?**

A: "We're purr-fect for each other!"

Q: **Why did the man put his car in the oven?**

A: He wanted to drive a hot rod.

Q: **How do you fix a broken vegetable?**

A: With tomato paste.

Q: **What did the buffalo say to his boy when he left for school?**

A: "Bi-son."

Q: What did the ice cream say to the bowl of soup?

A: "You melt my heart."

Q: How did the boulder go to bed?

A: He rocked himself to sleep.

Q: Why did the apple go to the gym?

A: To work on its core.

Q: What do you call it when the cafeteria burns the meat?

A: A mis-steak.

Q: Why did the mittens get married?

A: It was glove at first sight.

Q: Why was the dog laughing?

A: Someone gave it a funny bone.

Q: What do you get when you combine an apple and a tree?

A: A pine-apple.

Q: Why did the toad get sent to the principal's office?

A: It was a bully-frog!

Q: Why did the scientists fall in love?

A: They had great chemistry.

Q: Why don't you want to tell jokes to an egg?

A: You don't want it to crack up!

Q: Who borrows your Rollerblades all the time?

A: A cheap-skate!

Q: What do you get when an elephant runs through the cafeteria?

A: Squash!

Q: Why did the algebra teacher break up with the geometry teacher?

A: Something just didn't add up!

Q: What do bats do in their free time?

A: They just hang out!

Q: What do mallards watch on TV?

A: Duck-umentaries.

Q: What do you do when your dog eats your English paper?

A: Take the words right out of his mouth!

Q: Why did the couple eat fruit for breakfast every morning?

A: They wanted to live apple-y ever after.

Q: Why did the baby become a scientist?

A: She liked her formulas.

Q: What did the robin do when it got sick?

A: It went to the doctor for tweetment.

Q: Why did the kid carry a dictionary in his pocket?

A: He wanted to be a smarty-pants!

Q: Did you hear about the bedbugs that fell in love?

A: They are getting married in the spring!

Q: Where do swimmers go for fun?

A: To the dive-in movies.

Q: What do you call a sheep that does karate?

A: A lamb chop.

Q: Why did the computer stay home from school?

A: It had a virus.

Q: Where did the pigs go on their honeymoon?

A: New Ham-pshire.

Q: What do you call it when quarters

rain from the sky?

A: Climate change!

Q: What do you call a tuna in space?

A: A starfish.

Q: What did the slug say when he got

an A on his paper?

A: "I snailed it!"

Q: Why did the astronauts break up?

A: They needed some space.

Lisa: Why did Mom buy marshmallows?

Leah: She said we needed s'more.

Q: Why did the bug hide its trophies in the closet?

A: It was a humble bee.

Q: Why did the kid put his protractor in the refrigerator?

A: Because it was 180 degrees!

Q: Why did the girl break up with the baker?

A: Because he was a weir-dough!

Q: Why did the man's jacket catch on fire?

A: It was a blazer.

Q: What is a cat's favorite vegetable?

A: As-purr-agus.

Q: Why was the chicken late for school?

A: She didn't hear the alarm cluck.

Q: Why don't you want to date a meteorologist?

A: They always have their head in the clouds.

Q: Why did the cowboy take his horse to the vet?

A: It had hay fever.

Natalee: Did you enjoy your date with the surgeon?

Cheri: Yes, he had me in stitches the whole time.

Q: What do you get when you take a picture of a plant?

A: Photo-synthesis.

Q: Why do oysters make bad dates?

A: They always clam up on you.

Q: What gets harder to catch the faster you run?

A: Your breath.

Q: What can you serve but never eat?

A: A tennis ball.

Q: What does a cow pack in its lunch box?

A: Peanut udder and jelly sandwiches.

Q: What happened when the sea lions fell in love?

A: They sealed it with a kiss.

- -

Q: What do race car drivers eat before they race?

A: Car-bohydrates.

Q: What do you get when you cross Bambi and an umbrella?

A: A rain-deer.

Q: Why did the Skittles go to school?

A: They wanted to become Smarties!

Q: What did the baker wear on his date?

A: His new loaf-ers!

Q: What kind of shoes do butchers wear?

A: Meat loafers.

Q: Why was the insect so polite?

A: Because it was a ladybug.

Q: What happened when the janitor slipped on the wet floor?

A: He kicked the bucket!

Q: Why did the frogs get married?

A: They were toad-ally in love!

Q: **What happened when the skunk wrote a book?**

A: It became a best smeller!

Q: **What kind of birds end up in jail?**

A: Rob-ins!

Q: **What happened when the library flooded?**

A: It caused a title wave.

Q: **Why are painters so romantic?**

A: They'll love you with all their art.

Trapeze artist #1: Do you like your job at the circus?

Trapeze artist #2: I'm getting into the swing of things.

Q: What do you get when you cross a volcano and a vegetable?

A: A lava-cado!

Q: What do fish use for their lunch money?

A: Current-cy.

Q: What do you say if a porcupine gives you a kiss?

A: "Ouch!"

Q: What kind of fish likes bubble gum?

A: A blowfish.

Q: Why did the crow pick up the phone?

A: To caw, caw, caw somebody!

Q: Why was the triangle good at basketball?

A: It always made three pointers.

Q: Why shouldn't you date a mathematician?

A: They have too many problems!

Q: What happened to the boy who swallowed his trombone?

A: He tooted his own horn!

Q: Why don't you ever see elephants hiding in trees?

A: Because they're so good at it.

Q: Why did the jump rope get suspended?

A: It skipped school.

Q: Why did the girl have a crush on the fisherman?

A: He was quite a catch.

Mom: Do you think it will be a nice hotel?

Dad: I have reservations.

Q: Why are frogs always happy?

A: They eat what bugs them.

Q: Why can't you have class on an airplane?

A: Because your head would just be in the clouds.

Q: Why did the squirrels go on a date?

A: They were nuts about each other!

Q: Why wouldn't the sheep stop talking?

A: It liked to ram-ble!

Q: Why did the caterpillar go to so many parties?

A: It was a social butterfly.

Q: When is a mistake not a mistake?

A: When you learn from it!

- -

Q: What do you get when you cross Bigfoot and Shakespeare?

A: Romeo and Juli-yeti.

Q: What kind of clothes do dogs wear in the summer?

A: Pants.

Q: Why did the soccer player drop out of school?

A: He didn't have any goals.

Q: Why can't frogs get college degrees?

A: They croak before they finish.

Q: Why did the sharks get engaged?

A: They wanted to make it o-fish-al.

Tammy: Have you heard of the planet Saturn?

Timmy: It has a ring to it.

Q: What's a giraffe's favorite fruit?

A: A neck-tarine.

Q: Why can't elephants join the swim team?

A: They're always dropping their trunks!

Q: Why did the boy break up with the tennis player?

A: She made too much racket.

Lucy: How much is a pair of binoculars?

Lara: I'm looking into it.

Q: What kind of vegetable gets a pedicure?

A: A toma-toe.

Q: What is a witch's favorite subject in school?

A: Spelling.

Q: Why did the panther break up with the tiger?

A: She was always lion.

Q: What do you get when you put an opera singer in the bathtub?

A: A soap-rano!

Q: What do you get when you cross a fruit with a rock?

A: A pome-granite.

Q: Why did the kid fail his survival skills test?

A: It was too in-tents.

Q: Why don't you want to date a chicken?

A: They're cheep!

Q: Why can't you play hide-and-seek with mountains?

A: They're always peak-ing.

Q: What vegetable doesn't have any manners?

A: A rude-abaga.

Q: Where do surfers study?

A: In the board-room.

Q: When do you give astronauts their wedding presents?

A: At their meteor shower!

Q: Why are mountains always tired?

A: Because they don't Everest!

Q: What kind of bug never stops complaining?

A: A grumble bee.

Q: How did King Arthur finish his education?

A: He went to knight school.

- -

Q: Why did the farmer ask the florist to go on a date?

A: It was a budding romance.

Q: What are a horse's favorite snacks?

A: Straw-berries and hay-zelnuts.

Q: What kind of vegetable plays the drums?

A: The beet!

Q: Why was the broom late to school?

A: It over-swept.

Q: What did the worm say to her blind date?

A: "Where on earth have you been all my life?"

Q: What do you call a boomerang that doesn't come back?

A: A stick.

Q: What kind of candy will give you a rash?

A: Licor-itch.

Q: Why didn't the branch want to play at recess?

A: It was a stick in the mud!

Q: **Why did the girl turn down a date with the sailor?**

A: There was something fishy about him.

Q: **How does a bug get around in the winter?**

A: In a snowmo-beetle.

Q: **What do you get if you cross candy and balloons?**

A: Lolli-pops!

Q: **Why wouldn't the two 4's go out for dinner?**

A: Because they already 8.

Q: Why is it a bad idea to date a firefly?

A: They need to lighten up!

Q: How does a skater cut up her steak?

A: With Roller-blades!

Q: Why did the lemon marry the lime?

A: It was his main squeeze.

Q: Why did the horse go to the guidance counselor?

A: It wasn't feeling very stable.

Q: **Why does a mushroom have a date every weekend?**

A: He's a fungi!

Brayden: Have you seen bigfoot?

Hayden: Not yeti!

Q: **What do you call a cabbage on a plane?**

A: A vegetable with its head in the clouds.

Q: **Why didn't the moon eat all of its lunch?**

A: Because it was full.

Q: What do you get when you cross a dog and a dozen roses?

A: Collie-flower!

Q: Why did the guitar player go to the auto mechanic?

A: She needed a tune-up.

Q: What is the most adorable kind of bug?

A: A cuter-pillar.

Q: **What kind of dogs do they let into the library?**

A: Hush puppies.

Q: **Where did the cats go on their date?**

A: Out for mice cream.

Q: **What does an astronaut do with a bar of soap?**

A: She takes a meteor shower!

Q: **What is orange and sounds like a parrot?**

A: A carrot.

Q: What is a boa constrictor's favorite subject?

A: World hissss-tory.

Q: Why did the potato break up with the radish?

A: He was a dead-beet.

Q: Why was the whale always painting?

A: It was art-sea.

Q: What kind of mint is bad to eat?

A: A var-mint.

Jordan: How are your scuba-diving lessons going?

Justin: Swimmingly!

Q: What did the lipstick say to the eye shadow after their fight?

A: "Let's kiss and makeup."

Q: How does a lobster like its eggs?

A: With a pinch of salt.

Q: Where do hunters like to shop?

A: Target.

Q: How did the cows get to school?

A: On a com-moo-ter train.

Q: What do you get when you cross a bike and a bouquet of roses?

A: Flower pedals.

Q: Why did the whale need a hug?

A: It was blue.

Q: What do bugs write on?

A: Flypaper.

Q: Why did the almond go to the principal's office?

A: It was going nuts!

Q: What kind of drink is never ready on time?

A: Hot choco-late

Q: Why did the baker make so much bread?

A: Because it was kneaded.

Q: What do you call a wasp that doesn't cost anything?

A: A free-bee.

Q: Why don't rivers ever run out of lunch money?

A: They're always by the banks.

Q: Why did the girl break up with the trumpet player?

A: He was always tooting his own horn.

Q: What do sharks eat for breakfast?

A: Muf-fins.

Q: When do fish swim away and hide?

A: On Fry-days!

Q: How did the bull pay for his lunch?

A: He charged it!

Q: Why did all the girls have a crush on the guitar player?

A: He pulled on their heart strings.

Q: Why did the driver squeeze his car?

A: Because it was a lemon.

Q: What kind of animal doesn't have a name?

A: The anony-moose.

Q: What do you call a school on a mountain?

A: A high school!

Q: **Where did the rabbits go after their wedding?**

A: On their bunny-moon.

Q: **How many skunks does it take to change a light bulb?**

A: Just a phew.

Q: **What do you call a scarecrow that follows you everywhere you go?**

A: A corn stalker!

Q: **Why did the kids get stung at school?**

A: There was a spelling bee.

Q: When did Sir Lancelot go on a date?

A: At knight time.

Q: What do you get when you put glue on your doughnut?

A: A paste-ry.

Q: What do you get when you cross a dog and a bug?

A: A butterflea!

Q: Why did the car have excellent handwriting?

A: He had fine motor skills.

Q: How did the orange make time for his date?

A: He squeezed it in.

Q: What makes a pirate angry?

A: When you take away the *P*.

Q: What kind of bug is always on time?

A: A clockroach.

Q: Why wouldn't the skeleton try to learn at school?

A: It was a numbskull!

Q: Why did the boy go hunting with his date?

A: Because it only cost him a buck.

Q: What word has three letters and starts with gas?

A: A car.

Q: What do you get when you cross a cricket and a lawn mower?

A: A grasshopper!

Q: Why did the girl need a saddle to do her homework?

A: She was horseback writing.

Q: Why did the boy want to date the professional skier?

A: She had a hill-arious sense of humor!

Q: Why did the girl join the soccer team?

A: She thought she'd get a kick out of it.

Q: Why did the book join the FBI?

A: It wanted to go undercover.

Q: Why did the girl play her drum outside?

A: She wanted to beat around the bush.

Q: Why did the fish break up with the lobster?

A: Because he was shellfish.

Q: Where do you put fish once you catch them?

A: In a cof-fin.

Q: Why was the jelly late to school?

A: It got stuck in a traffic jam.

Q: Why were the golfers eating sandwiches and cake?

A: They were having a tee party.

Q: What is the best day to take your date to the beach?

A: Sun-day!

Q: Why don't crocodiles ever get lost?

A: They're great navi-gators.

Q: What kind of snake is good at math?

A: A pi-thon.

Q: What do you get if you give a robin a paintbrush?

A: A picture that's worth a thousand worms.

Q: Why did the girl have a crush on a skeleton?

A: Because he was humerus.

Q: What do a judge and a tennis player have in common?

A: They both go to court every day.

Q: Why aren't trees good at taking tests?

A: They're always stumped!

Q: How do you stop a dog in its tracks?

A: Hit the paws button.

Q: What did the rope do after it got engaged?

A: It tied the knot.

Q: What kind of fruits do boxers eat?

A: Black-and-blue berries.

Q: What kind of bugs are good at math?

A: Account-ants.

Q: What did the meteorologist do when she broke her leg?

A: She put it in a fore-cast.

Q: Why did the snowflakes go on a date?

A: They were falling for each other.

Q: What do you call a ram that tells a lot of jokes?

A: A silly goat.

Q: How did the brontosaurus feel after soccer practice?

A: Dino-sore.

Q: Why can't you win a race with a lettuce?

A: They always have a head start.

Q: What do you get when you cross headphones and roses?

A: Earbuds!

Q: Why did the fisherman run out of money?

A: He couldn't keep his business afloat.

Q: Why did the frog join the track team?

A: It was good at tadpole-vaulting.

Q: Why was the little bean crying?

A: It wanted its eda-mommy.

Q: Why did the bird get sick after its dinner date?

A: It had butterflies in its stomach.

Q: Why wouldn't the bike wake up?

A: It was two tired.

Q: What kind of dog is never late to school?

A: A watch-dog.

Q: What does a snake like to wear?

A: Ser-pants!

Q: How did the mermaid feel when she dated a human?

A: Like a fish out of water.

Logan: I caught fifty trout with just one worm.

Megan: That sounds a little fishy!

Q: Why do the marching-band members have such clean teeth?

A: They always have a tuba toothpaste.

Q: Why was the robin eating cake?

A: It was its bird*th*-day.

Q: What did one light bulb say to the other?

A: "I love you a watt!"

Q: What is a skunk's favorite color?

A: Pew-ter.

Q: Why did the chicken join the marching band?

A: It already had two drumsticks.

Q: What is a mallard's favorite game?

A: Duck, duck, goose.

Q: What happened when the drummer fell in love?

A: His heart skipped a beat!

Q: Why did the detective fall asleep at his desk?

A: He had a pillow-case.

Q: What is a kid's favorite day of the week?

A: Fri-yay!

Q: How did the dog know its owner was calling?

A: It had collar ID.

Q: What do you call two polar bears on a date in Hawaii?

A: Lost.

Andy: There's a skunk in my tent!

Mandy: That stinks.

Q: Why didn't anyone use the skunk's ideas for the science project?

A: Because they stunk!

Q: What kind of batteries should you bury?

A: Dead ones.

Q: What happened when the pigeons fell in love?

A: They were lovey-dovey.

Q: Why did the girl take a blender on a hike?

A: So she could make trail mix.

Q: Why did the boy get kicked out of band?

A: He always got in treble.

Q: How did the skunk go sightseeing?

A: In a smell-icopter.

Q: Why did the chicken break up with the rooster?

A: He had a fowl mouth!

Q: What kind of bird builds skyscrapers?

A: The crane.

Q: Why did the guitar hate going to band practice?

A: It was always getting picked on!

Janey: Do you want to look for fossils with me?

Jamie: I dig it!

Q: **What did the dairy farmer say to his wife?**

A: "You're my butter half!"

Q: **How much did it cost to build the beaver dam?**

A: An arm and a log.

Q: **What did the United States say to France at midnight?**

A: "Europe too late and you have school tomorrow!"

Q: **Why did the banana join the gymnastics team?**

A: It wanted to do the splits.

Q: Why does your grandma give the very best presents?

A: Because she's gifted.

Q: Why didn't the fisherman get his email?

A: He was out of net-work.

Q: Why don't kids in the choir get good grades?

A: They only go for the high C's.

Q: What is a tree's favorite vegetable?

A: Oak-ra.

Q: What did the horse do when she fell in love?

A: She got mare-ried.

Jerry: My campsite is better than yours!

Larry: Don't be so pre-tent-ious.

Q: Why don't fish get a summer vacation?

A: Because they're always in school.

Q: Why did the spider leave candy wrappers all over the ground?

A: It was a litter-bug.

Roger: Did you hit my car on purpose?

Roper: No, it was just a coinci-dents.

Q: Why do dragons sleep during the day?

A: They like to fight knights.

Q: What is the worst kind of candy?

A: Homework assign-mints!

Q: What do you get when you cross a spider and a computer?

A: A web-site!

Q: How do light bulbs send love letters?

A: By lamp-post.

Q: Why did the rabbit ride the roller coaster?

A: It was looking for a hare-raising experience!

Q: What is a whale's favorite thing to do on the playground?

A: The sea-saw.

Q: How did the zookeeper open the cage?

A: With a mon-key.

Q: **What time did the dentist pick up his date?**

A: Tooth-thirty.

Q: **What do rhinos and credit cards have in common?**

A: They both like to charge!

Q: **Why was the cow so popular?**

A: Because it was adora-bull.

Q: **When do they party in the castle?**

A: All knight long!

Q: What kind of flowers make great friends?

A: Rosebuds.

Q: Why did the boy wear a lampshade for a hat?

A: He felt light-headed.

Rita: Can you tell me if you brushed your teeth this morning?

Lisa: No, it's confi-dental.

Marney: What happens if bigfoot steps on your toe?

Millie: He'll Sasquatch it.

Gary: Did you see the movie about the unicorn?

Mary: I'd never myth it!

Q: Where do you find flying rabbits?

A: The hare force.

Q: Why did the kid want to study only sharks?

A: He was a fin-atic!

Q: What do you get when you combine a fish and a camel?

A: A humpback whale.

Q: Why was the nose still single?

A: It was too picky.

Q: What did the chef say after he cooked the steak?

A: "Well done!"

Q: What time is it when an elephant sits at your desk?

A: Time to get a new desk!

Q: When does a snake make you laugh?

A: When it's hiss-terical.

- -

Q: Why did the girl break up with the astronaut?

A: He was a bit spacy.

Bob: Did you hear about the farmer who wrote a joke book?

Bill: No, is it any good?

Bob: The jokes are pretty corny!

Q: How do smart students get to college?

A: On scholar-ships!

Q: What kind of shoes do frogs wear to the beach?

A: Open-toad shoes.

Q: What's the funniest time of day?

A: The laughter-noon!

Q: Why did the girl break up with the pastry chef?

A: He kept waffling.

Q: Why don't bakeries let their employees shave?

A: Because they need their whisk-ers.

Q: How do clams call their parents after school?

A: They use their shell phones.

Q: Why is the baker so lazy?

A: He's always loaf-ing around.

Q: What did the buck say to the doe?

A: "I'm fawned of you, deer."

Josh: Do you think change is hard?

Joe: I sure do! Have you ever tried to

bend a quarter?

**Q: What is an astronaut's favorite

part of the school day?**

A: Launch time!

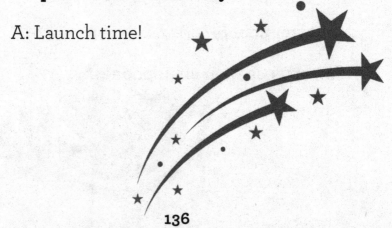

Q: What do baseball players and foxes have in common?

A: One catches fouls and the other catches fowls.

Q: Why did the girl agree to go out with the dentist?

A: She didn't want to hurt his fillings.

Q: Why don't dogs go to school?

A: They don't like arithme-tick.

Patient: Doctor, I think I broke my leg in two places! What should I do?

Doctor: Don't go to those places!

Q: Where does a bee wait for a ride?

A: At the buzz stop.

Q: What kind of bugs work at the bank?

A: Fine-ants.

Q: What do you get if you give diamonds to an ambassador?

A: Peace and carats.

Q: Why did the owl become a comedian?

A: Everyone said he was a hoot!

Q: How do you know if someone ran into your car?

A: Look at the evi-dents.

Q: Where do you mail your clothes?

A: To your home ad-dress.

Q: What do you call a bottle of free perfume?

A: Un-cent-ed!

Q: How is a professor like a thermometer?

A: They both have degrees.

- -

Q: Why did the tooth fairy fall in love with the sandman?

A: She thought he was dreamy.

Q: Why did the train go to the playground?

A: To blow off some steam.

Q: Why did the boxer punch his oatmeal?

A: He was making his break-fist.

Q: Why did the meteorologist go home?

A: He was feeling under the weather.

Q: What did George Washington call his false teeth?

A: Presi-dentures.

Q: How did the mad scientist cause a blizzard?

A: He was brain-storming.

Q: What do you call the selfie championships?

A: Olym-pics.

- -

Q: Why did quarters start falling from the sky?

A: There was change in the weather.

Q: What did one beekeeper say to the other?

A: "Mind your own buzz-iness!"

Q: What do you call a cow doing yoga?

A: Flexi-bull!

Q: Why did the boy have a crush on the baker?

A: She was a cutie-pie.

Q: What do you call it when you pass out the cards?

A: Ideal.

Q: What's the best time to get married?

A: On a Wednesday!

Q: How do you stay happy when you're running a marathon?

A: One s-mile at a time!

Q: Why did the dog get expelled?

A: It was a pit bully!

Q: Why did the referee jump in a puddle?

A: He wanted to wet his whistle.

Dave: Did you like my joke about the fish?

Adam: Not really.

Dave: Well, if you can think of a better fish joke, let minnow!

Q: Why can't fishermen get along?

A: They're always de-baiting!

Q: Why did the boy take the girl out for coffee?

A: He liked her a latte.

Q: Why did the astronaut leave the party?

A: He needed some space.

Q: How do you clean a pumpkin?

A: In a squashing machine.

Stanley: What happened when you found out your toaster wasn't waterproof?

Dudley: I was shocked!

Q: How does a witch doctor stay in shape?

A: They hex-ercise!

Q: What do you get when you cross a soda and a radio?

A: Pop music!

Patient: Doctor, I think I'm turning into a piano.

Doctor: Well, that's just grand!

Q: Why did the doctor become a brain surgeon?

A: He wanted peace of mind.

Q: Why did the surfer quit her job?

A: She wouldn't get on board.

Q: Did you hear about the couple who fell in love at the Indy 500?

A: Their hearts were racing!

Q: When must you open the door?

A: When you're obligated.

Q: What does it take to work for the railroad?

A: On-the-job training.

Q: **Why won't lobsters laugh at my jokes?**

A: Because they're crabby!

Jenny: I should give my pig a bubble bath.

Johnny: That's hogwash!

Q: **Why did the pirate share his secret treasure?**

A: He wanted to get it off his chest.

Q: **Why was everybody laughing at the mountain?**

A: Because it was hill-arious.

Jim: I need someone to help me build an ark.

Bob: I think I Noah guy!

Q: When is a nurse an artist?

A: When she is drawing blood.

Q: Where do cows display their homework?

A: On the bull-etin board.

Q: Where does a farmer stay on vacation?

A: At a hoe-tel.

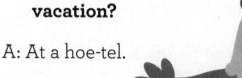

Q: **What do you call soap wearing a tuxedo?**

A: A detergent!

Jimmy: That soda just hit me on the head!

Bobby: Oh no, are you OK?!

Jimmy: Yeah, luckily it was a soft drink.

Q: **How does the sun say hello?**

A: With a heat wave!

Q: **Why did the skunk have to stand in the corner?**

A: It was a little stinker!

Q: What do night crawlers do before they go for a run?

A: Worm-ups.

Q: How do you feel when your shirt is wrinkled?

A: Depressed!

Tim: Hey, Mark. You want to hear my underwear joke?

Mark: Is it clean?

Q: What is a frog's favorite breakfast?

A: Toad-st and jam.

Q: Who says bad words at the store?

A: A cuss-tomer.

Q: How do you pay for the truth?

A: With a reality check.

Emma: Did you like your book about gravity?

Leah: Yes, I couldn't put it down!

Q: Where can you read about coffee cups?

A: In a mug-azine!

Q: Where can you read about insomnia?

A: In a snooze-paper.

Preston: Why did all the chickens disappear?

Winston: I don't have any eggs-planation!

Q: What do you call a book with sparkles?

A: Glitter-ature!

Q: What do you call a bunch of cows that live together?

A: A com-MOO-nity

Q: What did the mountain say to the valley?

A: "You're gorges!"

Q: What was Beethoven's favorite vegetable?

A: Bach choy!

Jenny: How was your date with the baseball player?

Jan: He knocked it out of the park!

Q: Where do heroes buy their food?

A: The super-market!

Q: **What kind of bird lives in a mansion?**

A: An ostrich!

Q: **What kind of fruit do you find in a volcano?**

A: A lava-cado!

Q: **Why couldn't the cat go on the field trip?**

A: It didn't have a purr-mission slip.

Q: **What did one woodworker say to the other?**

A: "I have a whittle crush on you!"

- -

Q: How do you know which flag is the best?

A: You take a pole.

Q: How do you feel when a giant lizard steps on your toe?

A: Dino-sore!

Q: What's the funniest fish?

A: A piranha-ha-ha!

Q: Why was the cat afraid of the tree?

A: It was a dogwood.

Q: Where should a wildcat sleep?

A: Behind a chain-lynx fence!

Q: Why did the ape ask for lemons?

A: So it could be orangu-tangy!

Q: What do you call a cat that wants to be a nurse?

A: A first aid kit-ten.

Q: Why did the surfer go to the salon?

A: She wanted a permanent wave.

Q: How do you buy a tropical fish?

A: With ane-money!

Jane: Where did you get your backpack?

Kate: That's a purse-inal question!

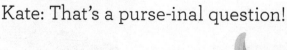

Q: What did the nurse say to the doctor?

A: "ICU!"

Q: How do you get your mom to make you some toast?

A: Just butter her up!

Q: What does a baker do for fun?

A: Bun-gee jumping!

Q: What do you get when paper towels fall asleep?

A: Napkins!

Bill: Did you like the sausage I cooked for you?

Joe: No, it was the wurst!

Q: What's a lawn mower's favorite music?

A: Bluegrass!

Q: How do you wash your stockings?

A: With a panty hose.

Q: Why did the vampire join the army?

A: So it could see combat!

Q: What do you give a dog who does extra homework?

A: Bone-us points!

Q: Why did the violin go to the gym?

A: So it could stay as fit as a fiddle.

Q: What does a baby ghost wear?

A: Bootees.

Q: What did one caramel say to the other?

A: "Let's stick together."

Q: What did the pig do when he wrote a book?

A: He used a pen name.

Q: What kind of flowers like to sing?

A: Pe-tune-ias.

Q: What happened to the singer after he was hit by lightning?

A: He became a shock star.

Q: Why did the gorilla stop eating bananas?

A: He lost his ape-tite.

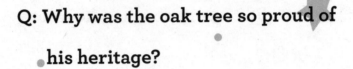
Q: Why was the oak tree so proud of his heritage?

A: Because his roots ran deep.

Q: Why did the boy throw branches in the lake?

A: He wanted fish sticks.

Q: How does a bumblebee get to school?

A: On the school buzz.

Q: Why does everybody like baby cows?

A: They're adora-bull!

Q: Why was the sailor upset over his report card?

A: His grades were at C level.

Q: What is a bird's favorite subject in school?

A: Owl-gebra.

Q: Why was the bacon laughing so hard?

A: Because the egg cracked a yoke!

Q: What did the sea lion say to the beaver?

A: "Will you be my significant otter?"

Q: What is a chimpanzee's favorite drink?

A: Ape-le juice.

Q: Why couldn't the Little Pig run away from the Big Bad Wolf?

A: He pulled a hamstring!

Q: Why can't you tell a whale anything?

A: It can't keep a sea-cret.

Q: What do you call a cobra without clothes?

A: S-naked.

Q: Why did the astronaut have to write everything down?

A: He just didn't have the brain space to remember things.

Q: What has a head and a foot but no arms?

A: Your bed.

Q: What do you call a really smart bug?

A: Brilli-ant!

Q: Why is the teacher in charge everywhere she goes?

A: She controls all the rulers.

Q: Why did the beaver cross the playground?

A: To get to the otter slide.

Q: What does Miss America drink?

A: Beau-tea!

Q: What do you call a locksmith that's in a bad mood?

A: Crank-key!

Q: Why don't dalmatians take baths before their dates?

A: They don't want to be spotless.

Ken: Do you like to eat venison?

Jen: It's deer-licious!

Q: Why did the skeleton's mom tell him to eat more?

A: Because he was boney.

Q: Why didn't the eagle practice flying?

A: She thought she could just wing it!

Q: Why did the panda join the choir?

A: He had a nice bear-itone!

Q: When is butter contagious?

A: When it's spreading!

Q: What is a monkey's favorite cookie?

A: Chocolate chimp.

Q: What kind of dessert do you eat in the bathtub?

A: Sponge cake.

Cowboy #1: Get the cattle! Get the cattle! Get the cattle!

Cowboy #2: I herd you the first time.

Pete: Did you hear about the guy who invented knock-knock jokes?

Dave: No, what about him?

Pete: He just won the no-bell prize.

Q: What is a wasp's favorite hairstyle?

A: A beehive.

Q: What happened when the television crossed the road?

A: It became a flat-screen TV!

Q: Why did the koalas get married?

A: Because life apart would be un-bear-able.

Tim: Did you hear the joke about the roof?

Mark: No, what is it?

Tim: Never mind. It's over your head.

Q: Why was the man running in circles around his bed?

A: He was trying to catch up on his sleep.

Teacher: Please use a pencil for this test.

Student: What's the point?

Q: What's an astronaut's favorite drink?

A: Gravi-tea.

Q: Where does spaghetti like to dance?

A: At the meatball.

Q: What did the paper say to the pen?

A: "Write on!"

Anne: Are you sure you want another cat?

Jane: I'm paws-itive!

Q: How does an angel light a candle?

A: With a match made in heaven.

Q: What do you get when you cross a turtle and a porcupine?

A: A slow-poke.

Q: What does the Queen of England like to wear?

A: A tea shirt.

Q: What muscle never says "hello"?

A: A bye-cep!

Q: What did the glue say to the paper?

A: "I'm stuck on you!"

Q: **Why was the snail too scared to leave its shell?**

A: It was spineless!

Q: **How many animals did Moses take on the ark?**

A: None, it was Noah's ark!

Q: **What do you call someone with an underwater race car?**

A: A scuba driver!

Q: **How do alligators give people a call?**

A: They croco-dial the phone.

- -

Jim: I have a henway in my pocket!

Joe: What's a henway?

Jim: About four or five pounds.

Sue: I finally got my new alarm clock.

Sal: It's about time!

Q: Why do monkeys like bananas?

A: They find them a-peeling.

Q: Where do cows go for lunch?

A: The calf-eteria.

Q: Why did the hot-air balloon get grounded?

A: It was getting carried away.

Q: Why was the cucumber so upset?

A: Because it was in a pickle.

Q: Why did the teacher take away the kids' soda?

A: They failed their pop quiz.

Q: What did the twig say to the log?

A: "I'll stick with you."

Q: What did the mommy elephant say to her baby?

A: "I love you a ton!"

Q: What do you call a crazy spaceman?

A: An astro-nut.

Q: How does it feel if a grizzly steps on your toe?

A: Unbearable!

Q: Why did the lettuce turn around?

A: It was headed in the wrong direction!

Q: Why did the chef quit making spaghetti sauce?

A: He ran out of thyme!

Q: Why did the orange juice get a bad grade on the test?

A: Because it wouldn't concentrate!

Q: What happened to the noodle that went down the drain?

A: He pasta way.

Q: What language do ducks speak?

A: Portu-geese.

Q: Why did the elephant quit the circus?

A: He was working for peanuts.

Q: When is music sticky?

A: When it's on tape.

Q: Where did the composer keep his sheet music?

A: In a Bachs.

Q: Why is it fun to date a farmer?

A: They're full of beans!

Q: What did the baker say to the bread?

A: "I knead you!"

Q: What kind of bread has a bad attitude?

A: Sourdough.

Q: Why is bowling like a flat tire?

A: You want a spare.

Q: What do you get if you're allergic to noodles?

A: Macaroni and sneeze.

Q: What do golfers drink out of?

A: Tee-cups.

Q: Why did the cow cross the playground?

A: To get to the udder slide.

Q: Why is it hard to have fish for dinner?

A: Because they're such picky eaters.

Q: Where do pigs keep their dirty clothes?

A: In the hamper.

Joe: Can you believe my dog caught a thousand sticks?

Jim: No, that sounds too far-fetched.

Q: Why don't dalmatians like hide-and-seek?

A: They're always spotted.

Q: What do you call an army of babies?

A: An infantry.

Q: Why did the girl break up with the butcher?

A: He was full of baloney!

Q: What do you call a shape that isn't there?

A: An octo-gone.

Larry: I dreamed about a billboard.

Lucy: I think it's a sign!

Q: Why did the spy come out at bedtime?

A: He only works undercovers.

Q: Why did the pig go into the kitchen?

A: It felt like bacon a cake.

Q: What do cats put in their iced tea?

A: Mice cubes.

Q: Why did the boy bring his piggy bank to football practice?

A: He wanted to be a quarter-back!

Q: What do monkeys eat for lunch?

A: Gorilla cheese sandwiches.

Q: Why did the music note drop out of college?

A: It couldn't pick a major.

Q: What do you get when you cross a horse and an angel?

A: A hay-lo.

Q: **What can you break without touching it?**

A: A promise!

Q: **What has to break before you can use it?**

A: An egg!

Q: **Did you hear about the runner whose date stood him up?**

A: His hopes were dashed!

Q: **What do sailors eat for breakfast?**

A: Boat-meal.

Q: Why did the monsters run out of food at their party?

A: Because they all were a-goblin.

Q: Why did the skier want to go home?

A: He was snow-bored.

Q: How does a farmer greet his cows?

A: With a milk shake.

Q: Why was the astronaut hungry?

A: Because he missed his launch.

Q: Why did the beaver study astronomy?

A: It wanted to go to otter space.

Q: What did the digital clock say to his mother?

A: "Look, Mom, no hands!"

Q: Why did the boy stop carving the stick?

A: He was a whittle tired.

Valerie: Do you feel better about yesterday?

Malorie: Yes, I'm past tense!

Q: Why did the can stop talking to the can opener?

A: Because he kept trying to pry.

Q: What did one egg say to the other egg?

A: "All's shell that ends shell."

Q: Why did the golden retriever have a crush on the poodle?

A: He thought she looked fetching.

Lou: What happened to all your furniture?

Sue: I gave it to chair-ity.

Q: What do you call a single person who's always wrong?

A: Miss-informed.

Q: What has eighteen wheels and running shoes?

A: A truck and fielder.

Q: What do you get when you cross a rabbit and a beetle?

A: Bugs bunny.

Q: What do sheep eat for breakfast?

A: Goat-meal.

Ben: My pants almost fell down!

Ken: That was a clothes call!

Q: How did the music teacher open her classroom door?

A: She used a piano key.

Q: What kind of car do dogs drive?

A: Land Rovers.

Q: What does a golfer eat for lunch?

A: A club sandwich.

Mary: How do you feel about your braces?

Molly: En-tooth-iastic!

Q: How do you get straight A's?

A: Use a ruler.

Q: Did you hear about the soccer players who broke up?

A: They were good sports about it.

Q: When do scuba divers sleep underwater?

A: When they're snore-kling.

Q: What do you get if you scare a tree?

A: Petrified wood!

Q: Why did the horse need a suitcase?

A: It was a globe-trotter.

Bella: You should write a book!

Stella: What a novel idea!

Q: What do you call it when candy canes decide to get married?

A: An engage-mint.

Q: What do you get when you bring your fishing pole to the library?

A: You get a bookworm!

Q: What do you call a happy cowboy?

A: A jolly rancher.

Q: Why did the pony ask for a glass of water?

A: He was a little horse.

Q: Why does grass have such low self-esteem?

A: It's always getting cut down.

Q: What kind of nuts are always catching colds?

A: Cashews!

Q: What do you get when you cross an owl with a magician?

A: Who-dini!

Q: What do you call it when farmers get married?

A: Grow-mantic!

Q: Why did the banker quit his job?

A: He lost interest.

Q: What kind of boat do you hit with a stick on your birthday?

A: A pin-yacht-a.

Q: How does a pirate clean his ship?

A: With a treasure mop!

- -

Q: Where did the whales go on their date?

A: To a dive-in movie.

Q: What happened when the rabbits got married?

A: They lived hoppily ever after.

Q: Why does the queen always hold an umbrella?

A: Because she reigns.

Q: What does peanut butter wear to bed?

A: Jammies.

Diner: This soup is too bland!

Chef: That's in-salt-ing!

Q: How do you find a train that is lost?

A: Follow its tracks.

Q: What kind of fruit is never alone?

A: Pears.

Q: How do you get an astronaut's baby to sleep?

A: You rocket.

Q: Why did the squash break up with the corn?

A: It was ear-ritating!

Q: How do you spot an ice-cream cone from far away?

A: With a tele-scoop.

Q: Why do you have to keep an eye on art teachers at all times?

A: Because they're crafty.

Q: Why do your little brothers always pick on you?

A: It's their expert-tease.

Q: Where do you keep a skeleton?

A: In a rib cage.

Q: How do you call an amoeba?

A: On a cell phone!

Q: Why is everybody running around?

A: They're part of the human race.

Jeff: We're getting a brand-new scale.

Steph: I can't weight!

Miley: Do you want to go fishing with me?

Alex: That's a fin-tastic idea!

Q: How do bugs feel about summer vacation?

A: Exuber-ant!

Q: What do you get when you cross a skunk and an elephant?

A: A smelly-phant.

Q: How does a mouse open the door?

A: With a squeak-key.

Q: Why did the girl have a crush on the sailor?

A: He was easy on the aye-ayes.

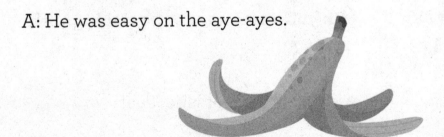

Q: Why don't stars carry luggage on vacation?

A: Because they're traveling light.

Q: Where do fairies go to the bathroom?

A: In the glitter box.

Q: What do you get when you give a rabbit a sleeping bag?

A: A hoppy camper!

Q: What do taxi drivers eat for dinner?

A: Corned beef and cabbage.

Q: Why was the dentist mad at the schoolteacher?

A: He kept testing her patients.

Q: What did the beach say to the wave?

A: "Long tide no sea!"

Q: What is a unicorn's favorite vegetable?

A: Horn on the cob.

Q: What is a sheep's favorite fruit?

A: Baa-nanas.

Q: Why did the early bird need a ruler?

A: It wanted to catch an inchworm.

Q: How do pandas fight?

A: With their bear hands.

Q: What do you get when you cross a robot and a pirate?

A: ARRRR2-D2.

Q: What did the butterfly say to the ladybug?

A: "You make my heart flutter."

Q: Why can't you trust a deer?

A: They'll always pass the buck.

Q: What kind of exercise should you do after you eat fast food?

A: Burpees.

Q: When do you bring a hammer on a hike?

A: When you want to hit the trail.

Q: Why was the frosting so stressed out?

A: It was spread too thin.

Q: Why did the horse put her foal to bed?

A: It was pasture bedtime.

Q: How do you know if a joke is about your mom and dad?

A: When the punch line becomes a-parent!

Amy: Do you like your new hair color?

Ellie: Yes, I've dyed and gone to heaven!

George: I finally finished raking the yard.

James: That's a re-leaf!

Sam: Did you like your karate class?

Marcus: I got a real kick out of it!

Q: How do you fix a squashed tomato?

A: With tomato paste.

Teacher: Do you know what caused the earthquake?

Student: I'm not sure, but it's not my fault!

Q: What did the dogs have to eat on their date?

A: Macaroni and fleas.

Q: What do you get when you cross a pine cone and a polar bear?

A: A fur tree.

Q: What do you get when you cross a toad and a pig?

A: A warthog.

Q: Why do sea turtles watch the news?

A: To stay up on current events.

Cassie: Do you like your astronomy class?

Kelly: It's out of this world!

Annie: I hear you got good grades in cosmetology school.

Lucy: Yes, I nailed it!

Q: Why did the cat smell so good?

A: It was wearing purr-fume.

Q: Why did the fawn put on a sweater?

A: Because it was buck naked!

Q: What do you give to a sick horse?

A: Cough stirrup.

Q: What did the horse put in its lunch box?

A: Straw-berries.

Carter: I want to have a space-themed birthday party.

Mom: Great, I'll planet!

Q: What did the stopwatch say to the clock?

A: "Don't be alarmed!"

Q: Why should you date a teacher when you grow up?

A: They have a lot of class.

- -

Q: What do you call a camel with no humps?

A: Humphrey.

Q: What do you call a stick of dynamite that keeps coming back to you?

A: A boomerang!

Q: Why are forest rangers so honest and reliable?

A: It's in their nature.

Q: How do marine biologists feel about the ocean?

A: They're fin-atics!

Q: Why did the boy eat waffles for breakfast, lunch, and dinner?

A: His mom said he needed three square meals a day!

Q: Why are tailors so funny?

A: They always have people in stitches.

Q: What do you call a horse in space?

A: A saddle-lite.

Q: How do you make a bug laugh?

A: Tickle it!

Q: Why do librarians move so fast?

A: They have to book it!

Q: When do sheepdogs cry?

A: When they're herding!

Q: What happened when the trees fell in love?

A: They got all sappy!

Q: Why is the shark still single?

A: It's too fin-icky!

Q: Where does a crocodile keep its milk?

A: In the refrige-gator.

Sam: Did you hear the principal wants to marry the school bell?

Joe: Yes, he gave it a ring!

Q: Does everybody drink soda?

A: It's pop-ular!

Q: What kind of dog uses a microscope?

A: A Labrador retriever.

Q: What do you call a sad cantaloupe?

A: Melon-choly.

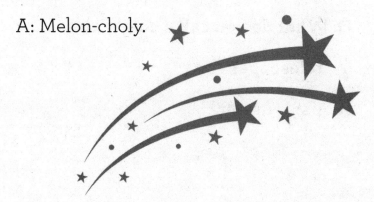

Q: Why did the bucket go to the doctor?

A: It was looking a little pail.

Joe: Why do you always cry at lunchtime?

Bill: Because we're in the cafe-tear-ia!

Amy: Did you hear about the atoms who were dating?

Annie: Yes, but I heard they just split!

Q: What do you call a cow with a telescope?

A: A star-grazer.

Q: What kind of clothes do houses wear?

A: Addresses.

Q: What did the conductor say to the misbehaving violin?

A: "You're in treble!"

Q: Why did the girl break up with the archer?

A: He was too arrow-gant.

Q: What does a soldier wear in the summer?

A: Tank tops.

Q: **What kind of shoes make fun of you?**

A: Mock-asins.

Q: **How does it feel to climb a mountain?**

A: Ex-hill-arating!

Q: **How many snails does it take to screw in a light bulb?**

A: Who knows? Nobody waits around long enough to find out.

Q: **What kind of animals make the best detectives?**

A: Investi-gators!

Leah: Did you hear about the kid who studied to be a mime?

Emma: No, what happened?

Leah: He was never heard from again.

Q: When doesn't a lamb spend any money?

A: When it's a sheep-skate!

Q: How does a blacksmith send a letter?

A: In an anvil-ope.

Q: Why did the camel decide to take up baseball?

A: So it could be a humpire.

Jimmy: Will you give me an abacus for my birthday?

Joey: Yes, you can count on it!

Charlie: Have you ever seen a catfish?

Jerry: Yes, but I don't think he caught anything.

Q: How do you get a cat to go out with you?

A: Be purr-sistent.

Q: Why did the carpenter quit using his drill?

A: Because it was always boring.

Q: Why did the carpenter become a comedian?

A: He had a really funny drill bit.

Q: When is a rabbit's foot unlucky?

A: When you're the rabbit.

Q: What do you call a mad biscuit?

A: A hot cross bun!

Q: Why did the baker study hard in school?

A: So he could make the honor roll!

Q: How do you make a bandstand?

A: Take away their chairs.

Q: Why did the meteor do well in school?

A: It was the teacher's star pupil.

Q: What do you call a friendly scoop of frozen yogurt?

A: Nice cream!

Q: Where did the pitcher dance with his girlfriend?

A: At the base-ball.

Q: Why did the rabbit go to the salon?

A: She was having a bad hare day.

Q: What do you get when you cross a dog and a crab?

A: A Doberman pincher.

Q: Why did the broccoli break up with the cabbage?

A: It had a big head.

Q: Why did the lumberjack chop down the wrong tree?

A: It was an axe-ident.

Q: Why did the chicken go to the gym?

A: It needed more eggs-ercise!

Tim: I hope they serve fish in the cafeteria.

Mark: I'm sure they will if the fish brings lunch money.

Q: Why did the egg get kicked out of the comedy club?

A: He was telling bad yokes.

Q: What do you get when you wear a watch for a belt?

A: A waist of time!

Q: How did the moon feel after lunch?

A: Full!

Jenny: Did you hear that grandparents are invited to school today?

Josie: That's old news!

Q: How do you motivate a lazy mountain?

A: Light a fire under its butte!

Q: How do you help out a baker?

A: Make a dough-nation.

Q: Why were the shoes still single?

A: They were de-feet-ed in love.

Q: What do bunny rabbits eat in the summer?

A: Hop-sicles.

Q: Why do cannibals like dentists the best?

A: They're the most filling!

Emma: Are you allowed to write a book?

Anna: Yes, I'm author-ized.

Q: How do you hide in the desert?

A: Wear camel-flage.

Q: What do you call a can of Jell-O?

A: Gelatin.

Q: What's the coldest letter in the alphabet?

A: Iced T.

- -

Tim: I forgot where I put my boomerang.

Scott: Don't worry, it'll come back to you!

Leah: Why do you have ten bowling balls?

Anna: So I'll always have one to spare.

Q: Why did the vegetable have to go to bed early?

A: It was just a little sprout.

Q: How did the celery get rich?

A: It invested in the stalk market.

Q: What do you get when you bring a rooster into the bathroom?

A: A cock-a-doodle-loo!

Q: What did the bulldozer say to the dump truck?

A: "I dig you!"

Q: Why did the baker have a rash?

A: Because he was making bread from scratch!

Q: What do you get when you walk your dog in Paris and it rains?

A: French puddles.

Q: What do you eat underwater?

A: Sub sandwiches.

Q: Why did the man stop at every service station on his way to work?

A: It isn't polite to pass gas.

Q: What do sailors like to read?

A: Ferry tales.

Q: Why did the bee go to the barber?

A: He wanted a buzz cut.

Dan: Can you help me find a new dentist?

Sam: You should try mine—he knows the drill!

Q: Why did the candy salesman put his phone in the freezer?

A: He had to make a few cold calls.

Josh: Let me tell you about my underwear.

Jeff: Okay, but please keep it brief. . . .

Max: What would happen if a snake swam across the Atlantic?

Jax: It would make hiss-tory!

Q: What did the bagel say to the bread?

A: "I like the way you roll!"

Travis: I was going to tell you a rumor about germs.

Scott: Why don't you?

Travis: I'm afraid it might spread.

Q: How does a deer carry its lunch?

A: In a bucket!

Q: What kind of car does the sun like to drive?

A: An S-UV.

Q: Why did the pig get out of bed?

A: It was time to rise and swine!

Q: What is E. T. short for?

A: Because his legs are so little!

Q: What do airplanes and football players have in common?

A: They both have touchdowns.

Q: Why did the bee need allergy medicine?

A: It had hives.

Q: What do you get when you cross a judge and a skunk?

A: Odor in the court!

Q: Who brings water to the baseball game?

A: The pitcher.

Q: Why did the wood fall asleep?

A: It was board.

Q: Why did the train need a tissue?

A: It was an achoo-choo train!

Q: Why shouldn't you take your date to the gym?

A: It might not work out.

Joe: Jim, does your doctor do house calls?

Jim: Yes, but your house has to be pretty sick before he'll come over.

Missy: What do you think of the Grand Canyon?

Mandy: It's gorge-ous!

Q: What do you call a stinky castle?

A: A fart-ress.

Q: Why did the boy stop using his pencil?

A: It was pointless.

Q: Why did the ruler fail in school?

A: It didn't measure up.

Q: Why did Mary's little lamb follow her to school?

A: It heard school was woolly fun.

Q: What kind of underwear does a lawyer wear?

A: Briefs.

Q: When does a hot dog get in trouble?

A: When it's being a brat.

Q: When can't you open the refrigerator door?

A: When the salad is dressing!

Parent: How was school today?

Child: There was a kidnapping in our class.

Parent: Oh, no! What happened?

Child: The teacher woke him up and gave him detention.

Q: Why don't frogs die from laryngitis?

A: Because they can't croak!

Q: How do skunks know if they're right for each other?

A: They trust their in-stinks.

Jen: Do you want to see the volcanoes in Hawaii?

Jill: I'd lava to!

Mason: Can we have a fish for dinner?

Lucas: Sure, I'll set an extra place at the table.

Q: Why was the astronaut crying?

A: He was a rocket-tear.

Q: What do you call a fake noodle?

A: An im-pasta.

Q: What has four legs but can't walk?

A: A chair.

Q: What do chickens play in the orchestra?

A: Bach, Bach, Bach.

Q: Why did the clam go to the gym?

A: To work out its mussels.

Sarah: Mom, can I plant flowers in the spring?

Mom: Yes, you May!

Q: How did the cat get the bread?

A: It baked it from scratch.

Q: Why didn't the Australian bear get the job?

A: It didn't have the right koala-fications.

Q: Why did the clock go back four seconds?

A: It was really hungry!

Q: Why did the monster get married?

A: He was the man of her screams.

Q: What is a skeleton's favorite instrument?

A: A trombone.

Q: Did you hear about the giant cow?

A: It's legen-dairy!

Q: What kind of bird is with you at every meal?

A: A swallow.

Q: What are a hyena's favorite cookies?

A: Snickerdoodles!

Q: What do you get when you cross Shakespeare and honey?

A: To bee or not to bee, that is the question.

Farmer: Why aren't my radishes growing?

Farmer's wife: Beets me!

Joel: Did you hear the joke about the strawberry jam?

Jill: Yes, it's spreading all over the place!

Q: Why did the baby snake cry?

A: Someone took away its rattle.

Patrick: Who can help me find a four-leaf clover?

Shannon: A lepre-can!

Q: What plays music in your hair?

A: A headband!

Q: What do you get when you cross a bee and a cupcake?

A: Fro-sting!

Q: Why did the hog have a stomachache?

A: He pigged out at dinner.

Q: Why did the stereo blow up?

A: It was radioactive!

Q: What did one atom say to the other?

A: "You matter."

Q: Why did they have to clean up the court after the basketball game?

A: All the players were dribbling.

Q: Why did the boy eat his homework?

A: Because the teacher said it was a piece of cake.

Q: What do you get when you throw noodles in a Jacuzzi?

A: Spaghetti.

Q: What do you get when you cross a frog and a clown?

A: A silly pad!

Q: Which tree is always at the doctor's office?

A: A sick-amore tree!

Lisa: Does your dog like its flea collar?

Anna: No, he's ticked off!

Q: Did you hear about the pilots who fell in love?

A: It was love at first flight.

George: What do snowmen wear on their feet?

Henry: Snowshoes!

Q: **What happens to toilet paper with good grades?**

A: It goes on the honor roll!

Q: **What do beavers put on their salads?**

A: Branch dressing.

Q: **Why don't grapes snore when they're sleeping?**

A: They don't want to wake the rest of the bunch.

Q: **What's a cow's favorite painting?**

A: The Moo-na Lisa.

Q: **What do you call a guy whose snowmobile breaks down?**

A: A cab

Q: **Why did the wheels fall over?**

A: They were tired!

Q: **What is a soda's favorite subject in school?**

A: Fizz-ics!

Q: **Why did the softball player save all her money?**

A: She was a penny pitcher!

Q: Where do you learn to saw wood?

A: In a boarding school.

Q: Where do you wash your hands in Hawaii?

A: In the lava-tory!

Sam: How do we know carrots are good for our eyes?

Emma: Have you ever seen a rabbit with glasses?

Q: Why did the banana put on sunscreen?

A: It was starting to peel.

Patient: Doctor, I think I'm a chicken.

Doctor: How long have you felt like this?

Patient: Since I was an egg.

Q: Why can't you trust a rubber band?

A: It's always stretching the truth!

Q: Which has more courage, a rock or a tree?

A: A rock, because it's boulder!

Q: What do you get when you cross a dentist and a boat?

A: A tooth ferry!

Ella: Mom, have you ever watched the movie *Bambi*?

Mom: Yes, deer.

Q: Why did the girl break up with the swimmer?

A: He went off the deep end.

Q: What kind of monster never irons its clothes?

A: A wash-and-wear-wolf.

Q: What do you call someone who grabs your cat and runs?

A: A purr snatcher.

Q: How did the orange cut in the lunch line?

A: It squeezed its way in!

Sam: Why did you bring your baseball bat to school?

Cam: It's time to hit the books!

Sadie: Did you hear about the couple who fell in love on an airplane?

Susie: Yes, because love is in the air!

Q: Why did the coffee bean stay home?

A: It was grounded.

Q: What is a tree's favorite drink?

A: Root beer.

Q: Where do you take a bad rainbow?

A: To prism.

Q: What did the pepperoni say to the mushroom?

A: "You stole a pizza my heart!"

Q: Why can't you trust artists?

A: They're sketchy.

Q: Why did the baseball coach go to the bakery?

A: He needed a batter.